MY BOOK OF
THE
PREHISTORIC
WORLD

Christopher Maynard and Chris Pellant

NEW YORK

KINGFISHER
Larousse Kingfisher Chambers Inc.
80 Maiden Lane
New York, New York 10038
www.kingfisherpub.com

Material in this edition previously
published by Kingfisher Publications Plc
in the **My Best Book** of series

This edition published in 2001

1 3 5 7 9 10 8 6 4 2
1TR/WKT/MA(MA)/0501/140MA

LIBRARY OF CONGRESS CATALOGING-IN-PUBLICATION DATA
has been applied for.

ISBN 0-7534-5400-9

Printed in Hong Kong

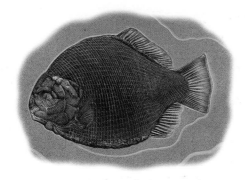

Contents

4 The age of the Earth

6 Our rocky world

8 Dinosaur babies

10 Bringing up baby

12 Living in herds

16 A gentle plant-eater

20 A fierce meat-eater

23 Going hunting

24 Pack attack!

28 Run for your life!

30 Then they were gone

32 Fascinating fossils

34 Layers of life

36 Clues to the past

38 Fossil hunters

40 Bone puzzle

42 Starting a collection

44 Glossary

46 Index

48 Places of interest and useful websites

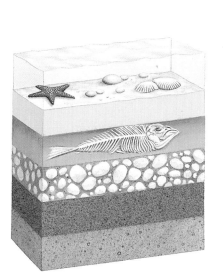

The age of the Earth

Our rocky planet is older than we could ever imagine. About 4,600 million years ago, the Earth was a huge, fiery ball circling the sun. Much of the surface was covered with hot, liquid rock—lava that poured out from volcanoes and meteorites that had crashed down from space.

Cooling down

Over millions of years, the surface began to cool and shrink. Inside the Earth, chemical substances called minerals joined together to make different kinds of rocks. A rocky crust formed on the outside. Today, the Earth's surface seems solid, but new rocks are constantly forming.

4

Our rocky world

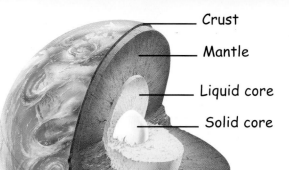

Crust
Mantle
Liquid core
Solid core

The rocks that we see today on the Earth's surface were formed in different ways. Geologists have discovered that all rocks belong to three main groups: sedimentary, igneous, and metamorphic. The names describe how the rocks were made— sedimentary means "made from sediment," igneous means "fiery," and metamorphic means "changed."

Under our feet

The Earth has a hard rocky crust. Below the crust lies the mantle, which is so hot that in some places the rock has melted. The core is even hotter and is made of both solid and liquid metal.

Made by fire

Many igneous rocks form when lava is forced out of an erupting volcano, and then cools and hardens on the surface.

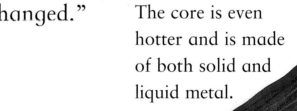

Layers of sediment

Sedimentary rocks are made
from sediments such as sand,
clay, and seashells that pile
up in layers in lakes, rivers,
and oceans. Over time, these
layers are pressed tightly
together to make solid rock.

Sedimentary rock layers in cliffs

Metamorphic rocks form mountains

Changed rocks

Metamorphic rocks form
in the ground when heat and
pressure change the structure
and appearance of igneous
and sedimentary rocks. The
changed rocks are pushed
up from under the ground
to form hills and mountains.

Dinosaur babies

Dinosaurs first appeared on Earth 230 million years ago. This Maiasaura mother dinosaur has been guarding her eggs for many weeks. Now, one by one, her babies crack through their shells and wriggle out into the huge nest. Some stop to nibble at the blanket of rotting plants that has been keeping them warm. Others peer over the lip of the nest to take their first look at the world.

Large, intelligent eyes

Troodon

Small, sharp teeth for grabbing and biting

Powerful arms and claws

Nest raiders

Unguarded eggs were often snatched by small, fast dinosaurs, such as Troodon, which hunted in packs.

Dinosaur eggs

Dinosaurs were reptiles and they all laid eggs, as reptiles do today. Some eggs were round, but most were long and fat. The biggest were the size of a football.

Chicken egg
3 inches long

Maiasaura egg
4¹/₂ inches long

Protoceratops egg
8 inches long

Hypselosaurus egg
11¹/₂ inches long

Bringing up baby

◀1 Most dinosaurs laid their eggs in nests. A few, like Maiasaura, built their nests together, in a group or colony. Every year, they went back to the same place to lay their eggs.

▶2 First, a Maiasaura mother dug a large, round hole. It was about the size of a backyard wading pool but much deeper.

◀3 Then she laid up to 20 eggs in the nest. Each egg was 4¹/₂ inches long and had a soft, leathery shell. The eggs rolled to the bottom of the nest, and the mother covered them with a thick layer of plants to keep them warm.

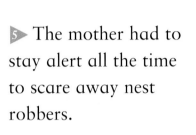

4 Day after day, the mother guarded her nest while the layer of plants rotted and kept the eggs warm.

5 The mother had to stay alert all the time to scare away nest robbers.

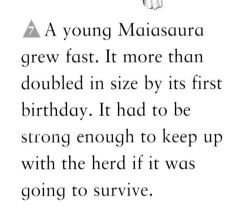

7 A young Maiasaura grew fast. It more than doubled in size by its first birthday. It had to be strong enough to keep up with the herd if it was going to survive.

8 The young dinosaurs stayed with the herd for the rest of their lives. Safety in numbers was their best defense against meat-eating dinosaurs that might attack and eat them.

6 Many weeks later, the eggs stirred, and cracked, and the first babies hatched. Within a few minutes they were able to walk around and forage for food.

Living in herds

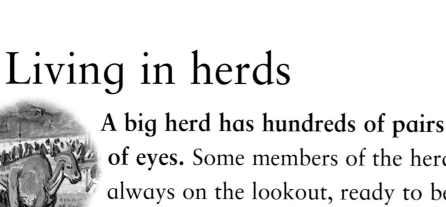

A big herd has hundreds of pairs of eyes. Some members of the herd are always on the lookout, ready to bellow a warning if they spot a hunter. Most of the dinosaurs that lived in herds were peaceful plant-eaters. If there was plenty of food, a herd might grow to a hundred or more.

This herd of duckbills is moving through a thick jungle of trees, shrubs, and ferns. As it passes, thousands of crunching teeth will strip the stems and trunks bare.

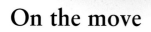

On the move
Some dinosaurs, like long-necked Apatosaurus, traveled hundreds of miles to find new feeding grounds.

Nose flap could be blown up like a balloon to honk

Edmontosaurus

Hollow horn

Tsintaosaurus

Bony ax-shaped crest

Lambeosaurus

Duckbilled dinosaurs

Duckbills had long, flat snouts, a little like a duck's bill. The scientific name for them is hadrosaurs. Most duckbills had bumps, horns, or crests on their heads, and males usually had larger horns or crests than females. They used them to hoot or honk to the rest of the herd. In this way, a duckbill could signal that all was well, or warn the herd of danger.

Guarding their young

When a herd of dinosaurs was on the move, like these Iguanodons, babies walked in the middle, guarded by their parents.

Pachycephalosaurus

Making a circle

Λ Triceratops herd backed into a circle if attacked, with babies in the center and big males pointing their horns outward.

Keeping watch

At night, dinosaurs settled down to sleep in a large herd. Some were always awake and moving around, like soldiers on guard duty.

Fighting one another

In some big herds, males fought one another for a female or to decide who would be head of the herd, just as deer do today.

A Pachycephalosaurus had a thick, dome-shaped skull to protect its brain during head-on fights. The males crashed into each other until the weaker one ran away.

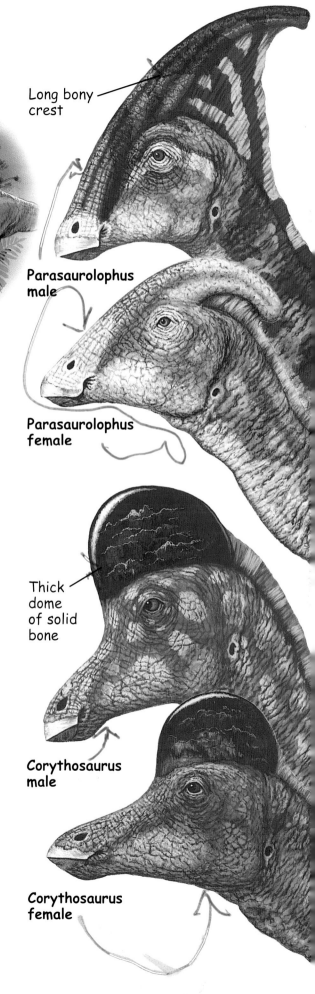

Long bony crest

Parasaurolophus male

Parasaurolophus female

Thick dome of solid bone

Corythosaurus male

Corythosaurus female

A gentle plant-eater

A giant head swings up, and the tall trees around it sway like grass. It strips a mouthful of juicy leaves and twigs with its stumpy, peg-shaped teeth. Then it swallows everything, without chewing, down a neck as long as a telephone pole.

This is Barosaurus—a giant plant-eater belonging to a group of long-necked dinosaurs called sauropods. Barosaurus was as tall as a five-story house. It needed to eat all day to fuel its huge body. But being huge made Barosaurus safe. Few hunters would dare attack anything so big.

Stomach stones

Big dinosaurs gulped down stones as they ate. The stones stayed in the gut, helping the stomach muscles grind leaves and twigs into a soft, sticky stew of plants. The dinosaur could digest this stew more easily.

16

Long-necked dinosaurs

Long-necked plant-eaters were the biggest animals ever. Next to them, an elephant looks tiny. To see how long Diplodocus was, loop some string around this book. Put the book on the floor, and take 130 short paces (each as long as your foot), unwinding the string as you go. Now look back. Could you fit one in your house?

Big foot

A long-neck's footprint was about 4 feet long— five times longer than yours. It walked at the same speed you walk.

Apatosaurus
80 feet long

Titanosaurus
45^1/$_2$ feet
long

Diplodocus
99 feet
long

18

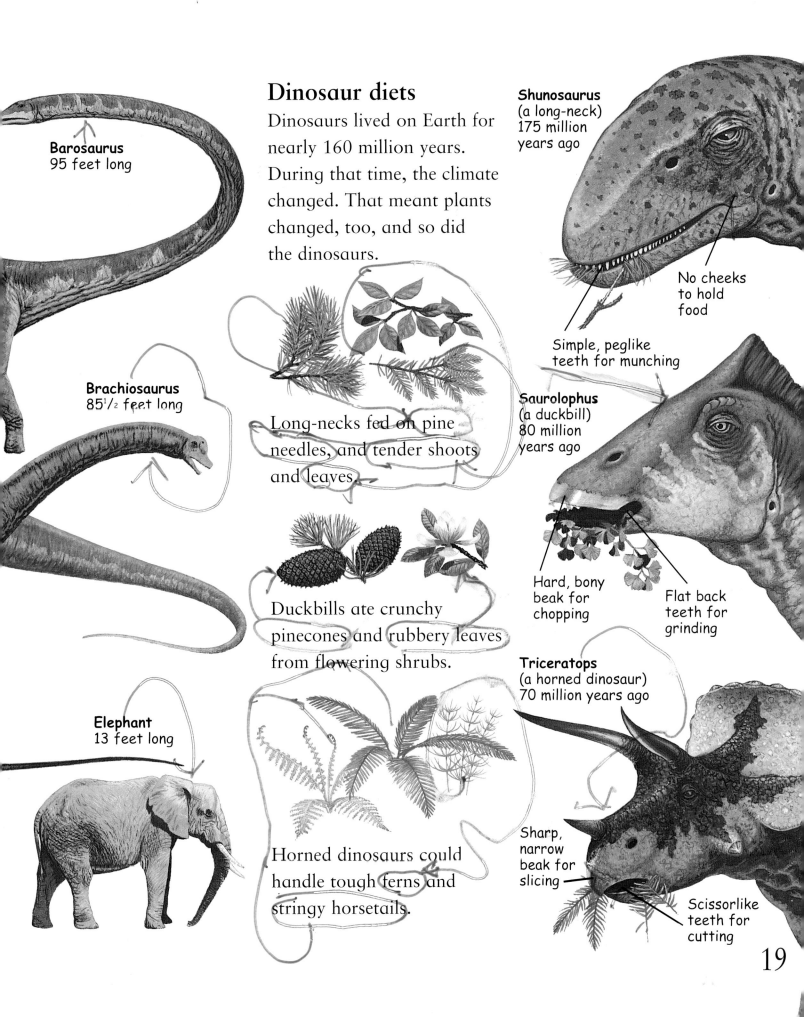

Barosaurus
95 feet long

Dinosaur diets

Dinosaurs lived on Earth for nearly 160 million years. During that time, the climate changed. That meant plants changed, too, and so did the dinosaurs.

Shunosaurus
(a long-neck)
175 million
years ago

No cheeks
to hold
food

Simple, peglike
teeth for munching

Brachiosaurus
85¹/₂ feet long

Long-necks fed on pine needles, and tender shoots and leaves.

Saurolophus
(a duckbill)
80 million
years ago

Duckbills ate crunchy pinecones and rubbery leaves from flowering shrubs.

Hard, bony
beak for
chopping

Flat back
teeth for
grinding

Triceratops
(a horned dinosaur)
70 million years ago

Elephant
13 feet long

Horned dinosaurs could handle tough ferns and stringy horsetails.

Sharp,
narrow
beak for
slicing

Scissorlike
teeth for
cutting

19

A fierce meat-eater

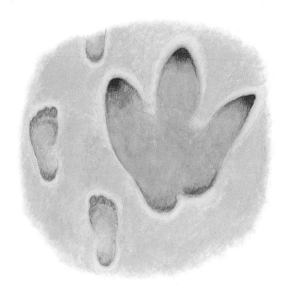

Lurking in the shadows of a redwood forest, the giant Tyrannosaurus sniffs the breeze and grunts. It can smell food nearby. Then it spies a mother Edmontosaurus and two youngsters at rest in a glade.

The big hunter stalks them quietly. Then, when it is just 380 feet away, it erupts from the trees like a roaring express train. In just a few seconds, well before its victims can rise and run away, it is on them. Its huge, heavy jaws tear into one of the young dinosaurs with a wild, killing bite.

Quick foot

This is Tyrannosaurus's footprint. It had three toes, with a giant talon on each toe. At two feet long it was twice as long as a human footprint.

Tyrannosaurus could run as fast as a horse, at almost 24 miles per hour.

Meet Tyrannosaurus

A full-grown Tyrannosaurus rex had about 50 razor-sharp teeth. Each tooth was as long as a banana.

It had a sharp point to stab its victim, and rough edges to rip through skin and flesh.

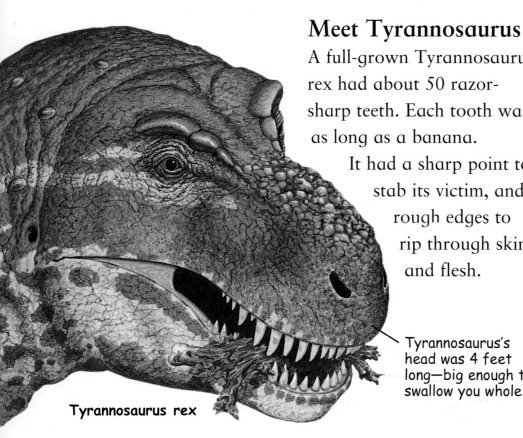

Tyrannosaurus rex

Tyrannosaurus's head was 4 feet long—big enough to swallow you whole

When old teeth wore out, new ones grew in their place

Allosaurus

Dilophosaurus

Albertosaurus

Big meat-eaters

These three fierce hunters were all related to Tyrannosaurus and had sharp teeth and claws. None, though, were quite as big. A full-grown Tyrannosaurus was tall enough to look through a second-floor window.

Going hunting

▶ **1** Allosaurus wakes up and rises slowly from the ground. It uses its small arms to balance as it rears up on its hind legs.

▼ **3** A few hours later, its sharp eyes spot a herd of plant-eaters. Slowly it creeps up on them, looking for a likely victim. Allosaurus waits, and waits, for just the right moment.

◀ **2** Its last meal was four days ago, and now it is very hungry. It finds an old carcass and tears at the bones, but there is little meat left to ease its hunger.

4 A young dinosaur foolishly lags behind the herd. Allosaurus bursts from its hiding place in a short, swift sprint and grabs its victim by the neck. Its fangs sink deep and tear out a huge slab of flesh in one lethal bite.

▶ **5** Allosaurus tears out chunk after chunk of flesh and bone and swallows them whole. It gorges till its belly is bloated. Then it staggers away to lie down and doze for hours, just like a well-fed lion.

Pack attack!

Sauropelta is bigger than a bison and bristling with armor, but the pack of Deinonychus still attacks.

The wolf-sized hunters charge at Sauropelta from all sides, trying to rake its hide with their fangs and slash open its underbelly with their giant claws. But their prey's hide is so studded with spikes, horns, and bony knobs that they don't do much damage.

One attacker is knocked to the ground by Sauropelta's swinging tail and is trampled in the dust. The ferocious pack will soon give up and search for an easier meal.

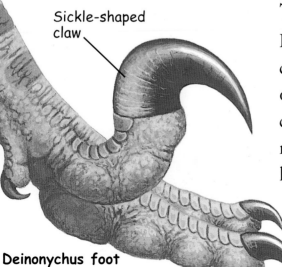

Sickle-shaped claw

Deinonychus foot

Terrible claw

Deinonychus had a huge claw on the second toe of each back foot. The claw swiveled up as it ran and swung down like a slashing knife blade when it attacked.

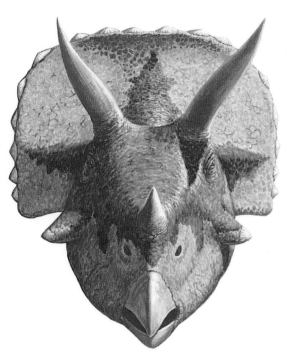

Triceratops

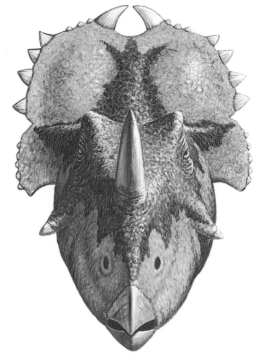

Centrosaurus

Chasmosaurus

Armored dinosaurs

Plant-eaters had many ways of protecting themselves. Some lived in herds and found safety in numbers. A few were just too big to be attacked. Others had body armor to defend themselves, and horns or spiked tails to fight with.

The three horned dinosaurs above had huge, bony neck frills. If an attacker tried to bite them, it would break its teeth.

Ankylosaurus was like a four-legged tank, with thick, leathery skin and bony lumps and spikes all over its head and back. If attacked, it crouched down to protect its underbelly.

Ankylosaurus

Heavy, clubbed tail

Bony spikes

Soft underbelly

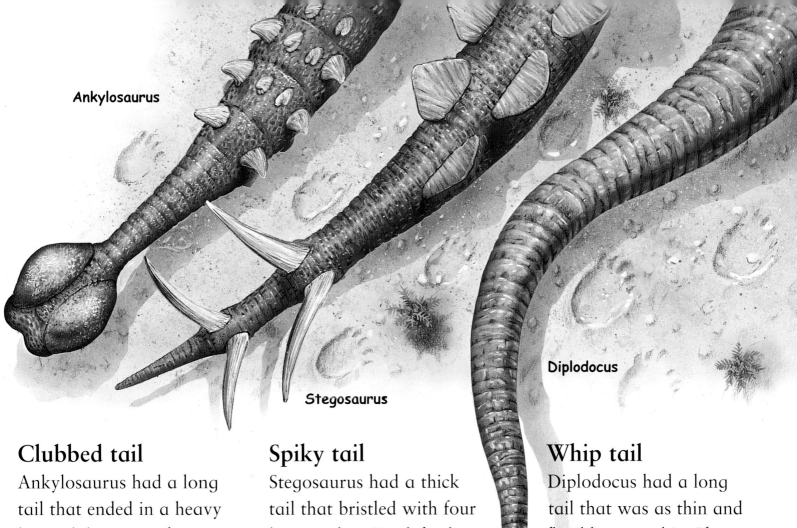

Ankylosaurus

Stegosaurus

Diplodocus

Clubbed tail

Ankylosaurus had a long tail that ended in a heavy bony club up to 4 feet wide. The dinosaur swung its tail at an attacker. One blow was powerful enough to shatter bone, or even kill.

Spiky tail

Stegosaurus had a thick tail that bristled with four large spikes. To defend itself, it turned its back on attackers and swung its tail back and forth to give a lethal blow.

Whip tail

Diplodocus had a long tail that was as thin and flexible as a whip. If attacked, it lashed it to and fro. Its weight could land a blow hard enough to knock an attacker off its feet.

Run for your life!

The sound of pounding hooves drums across an open plain as a herd of long-legged, ostrichlike dinosaurs runs for its life. Smaller dinosaurs like these didn't have horns or clubbed tails to protect them from meat-eaters. What they did have was speed. Struthiomimus was as fast as a racehorse and could outrun almost any attacker.

Freeze

Tiny Compsognathus used its speed to catch lizards or frogs. If hunted by a larger dinosaur, it hid and froze in the undergrowth.

Safety in numbers
Like other small plant-eaters, Lesothosaurus relied on the rest of its herd to spot danger, and on its speed to get away.

Raid and run
Oviraptor was fast enough to catch darting lizards or small mammals. It used speed and agility to escape from its enemies, too.

Run like the wind
Hypsilophodon was one of the fastest small plant-eaters. As it fled, it dodged from side to side to escape claws and jaws.

Then they were gone

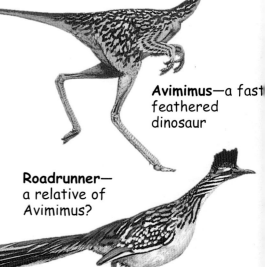

Avimimus—a fast feathered dinosaur

After ruling the world for 160 million years, all the dinosaurs died out. Why? It's most likely that the dinosaurs became extinct after a meteorite smashed into Earth, exploding with the power of a thousand volcanoes. The explosion burned and killed everything for thousands of miles. It also flung up enough dust to block out the sun's light and heat. Earth became cold, and many creatures—including the dinosaurs—perished.

Roadrunner—a relative of Avimimus?

Dinosaur survivors
Some scientists think that dinosaurs were the ancestors of modern birds.

1 A huge meteorite, 6 miles wide and traveling at 60,000 miles per hour, hit Earth in Central America.

2 It formed a crater almost 120 miles wide and threw a massive cloud of dust into the sky.

3 The dust blocked out the sunlight for many years. The air became cold. Many plants and animals died.

Fascinating fossils

How fossils form

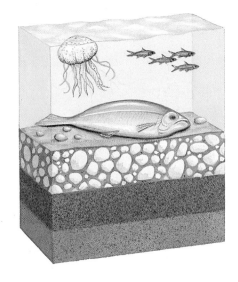

1 When a fish dies, its body sinks to the seabed. The soft parts of the fish rot away.

Fossils are the remains of plants and animals, such as dinosaurs, which may be millions of years old. Most fossils are discovered in sedimentary rock, in areas that were once in or near water, such as a sea or a river. They were formed after plants and animals died and were buried under layers of sediment. While the soft parts rotted away, the hard parts, such as shells, bones, teeth, and even whole skeletons, became fossils.

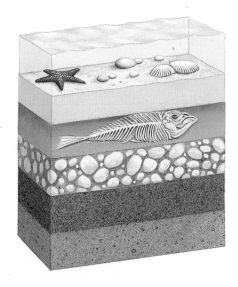

2 Gradually, the skeleton is covered with layers of sand and mud. This settles and becomes solid rock.

3 After millions of years, movements in the Earth bring the rocks containing the fossil above sea level.

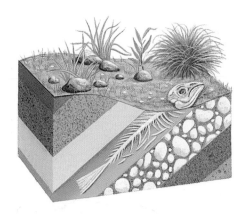

4 The rocks containing the fossil are worn away by the weather and the fossil is exposed on land.

Frozen in time

Not all fossils are found in stone. Some plants and animals are found as they were in life. There are many different ways in which fossils can be preserved.

Insects can be preserved whole in pine-tree resin. Over time, this turns into amber

Ice can preserve bodies. This baby mammoth was found frozen in the ice in Siberia, in Russia

The wood of this tree trunk has been replaced, molecule by molecule, by minerals that turned to stone. This is called petrification

This ancient leaf imprint is nearly 300 million years old. The original leaf was fossilized in layers of coal

This detailed fossil of an early fish has been preserved in stone

33

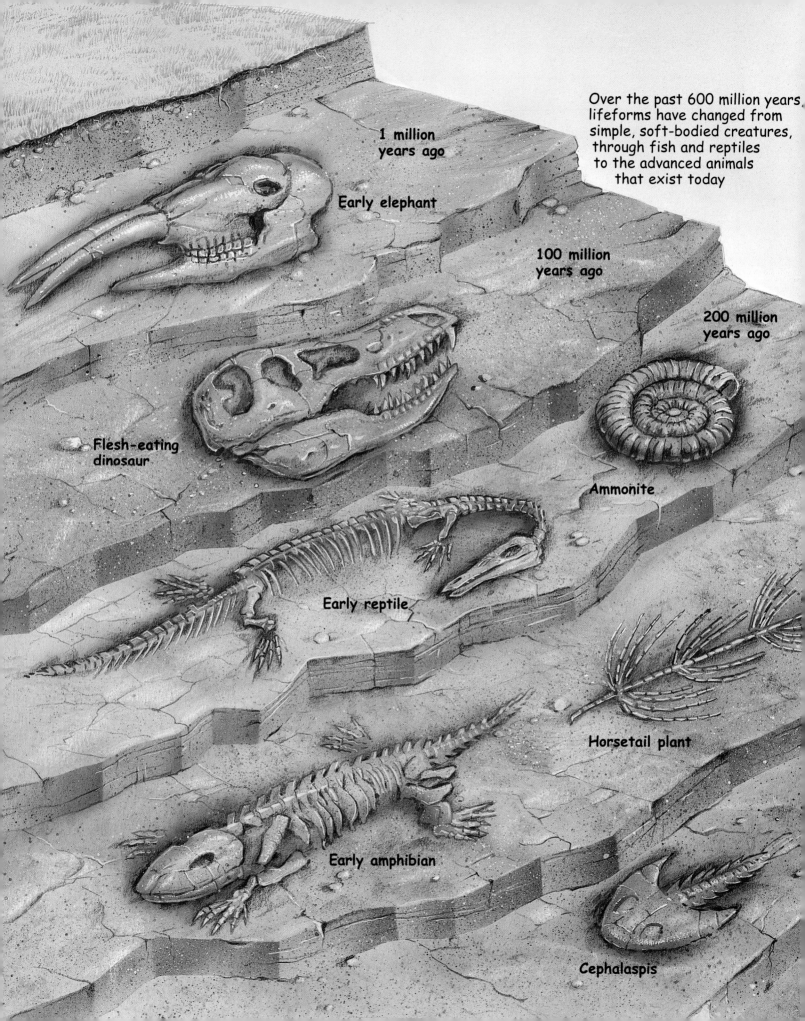

1 million years ago

Early elephant

Over the past 600 million years lifeforms have changed from simple, soft-bodied creatures, through fish and reptiles to the advanced animals that exist today

100 million years ago

200 million years ago

Flesh-eating dinosaur

Ammonite

Early reptile

Horsetail plant

Early amphibian

Cephalaspis

Layers of life

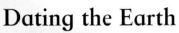

Millions of living things have existed on Earth, but only a small number of them ever became fossils.

Fossils are very important because they show how life on our planet has changed over many millions of years.

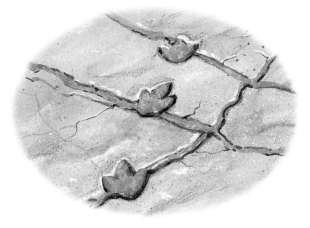

Dinosaur footprints in the rock

Dating the Earth

The Earth's history is divided into periods. Different creatures and plants lived at different times. Geologists can tell how old rocks are by studying the kinds of fossils that are found in them.

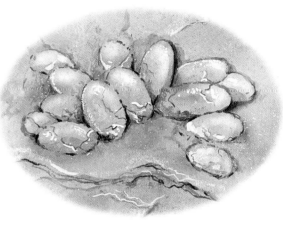

Dinosaur eggs found in China

Trace fossils

Fossils that show where animals have been are called trace fossils. Many large dinosaurs left fossilized footprints and eggs as evidence of where they once lived.

300 million years ago

400 million years ago

Early fish

500 million years ago

Trilobite

600 million years ago

Brachiopod

Ediacaran animal

Clues to the past

Evolution is the way in which animals and plants change over many generations. Fossils are clues about how life on Earth has evolved. They show us the links between many of today's species and their long-extinct ancestors. For example, by studying the Archaeopteryx fossils found in Germany, scientists discovered more about the ancient link between birds and reptiles.

Clawed climber

Archaeopteryx spent much of its time in trees, using the sharp claws on its feet and wings to climb.

A pair of
Archaeopteryx
climb above
the treetops

Archaeopteryx had razorlike teeth, ideal for eating prey like dragonflies

Winged wonder

Archaeopteryx was a poor flier and would have used its wide wings to glide from branch to branch or to swoop to the ground.

Missing link

In 1861, the discovery of the first Archaeopteryx fossil amazed scientists. They believed that it was the remains of a bird because it had feathers and wings. But it also had some reptilelike features such as sharp teeth, claws, scaly legs, and a long, bony tail. For the first time, a possible link between reptiles and birds had been found.

Fossil hunters

Discovering a new dinosaur site is an exciting event. The remains of these creatures have been found in remote places as far apart as the United States, China, Australia, and Britain. Occasionally, people have stumbled across dinosaur bones by accident. More often, the bones are found by geologists who know where to look.

Dinosaur dig

When a skeleton is unearthed, it has to be moved carefully because the bones are very fragile. The remains are then taken to a museum to be studied and put on display.

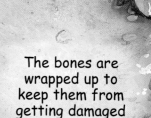

A brush is used to remove dust and sand from around the fossil

The bones are wrapped up to keep them from getting damaged

She sells seashells

This tongue twister is about Mary Anning, a young English fossil hunter. Early in the 1800s, she discovered the skeleton of an ichthyosaur near the sea in England. This was one of the first fossils of this marine reptile ever to be found, and she sold it for a large amount of money.

The geologists wear protective clothing and hard hats at all times while on the site

Rock is carefully removed from around the skeleton using special tools

A detailed drawing is made to show exactly where the bones were discovered

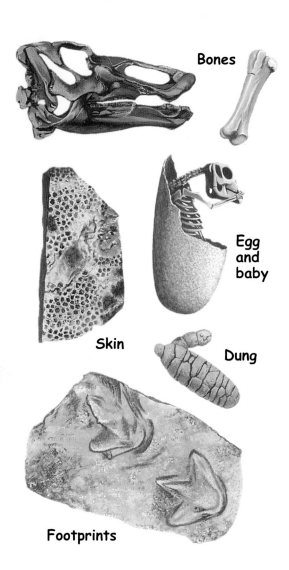

Bones

Egg and baby

Skin

Dung

Footprints

Bone puzzle

1 When the fossils have been moved to a museum, they are broken out of their plaster cases with saws, hammers, and chisels.

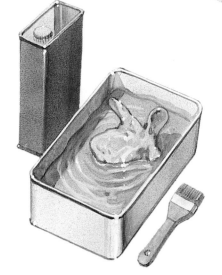

2 If the fossil has been lying in a rock called limestone, it may be given a bath in weak vinegar to help to wash away some of the limestone rock.

All kinds of fossil

Scientists do not only find fossils of bones. Far more often, they find fossils of footprints. Their size and how far apart they are tell us how big and how fast the dinosaur was. We also have fossils of dinosaur eggs and, sometimes, fossils that show scaly skin. We even have fossils of dinosaur dung!

3 Dentist's drills, toothpicks and magnifying glasses are used to clean the last traces of rock from each bone. A dinosaur has over 300 bones, so it can take months to do this delicate job.

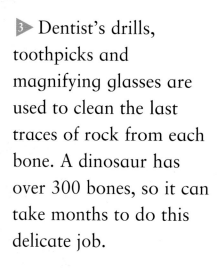

4 ▶ Fossils are old and can easily crumble. Scientists paint them with special chemicals to stop them falling apart, and to protect them from dust and dirt.

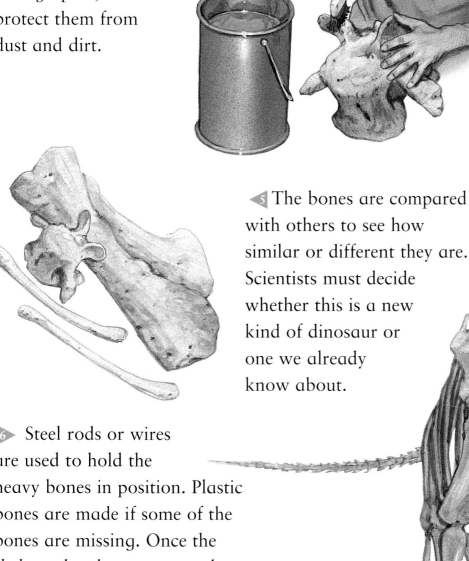

5 ◀ The bones are compared with others to see how similar or different they are. Scientists must decide whether this is a new kind of dinosaur or one we already know about.

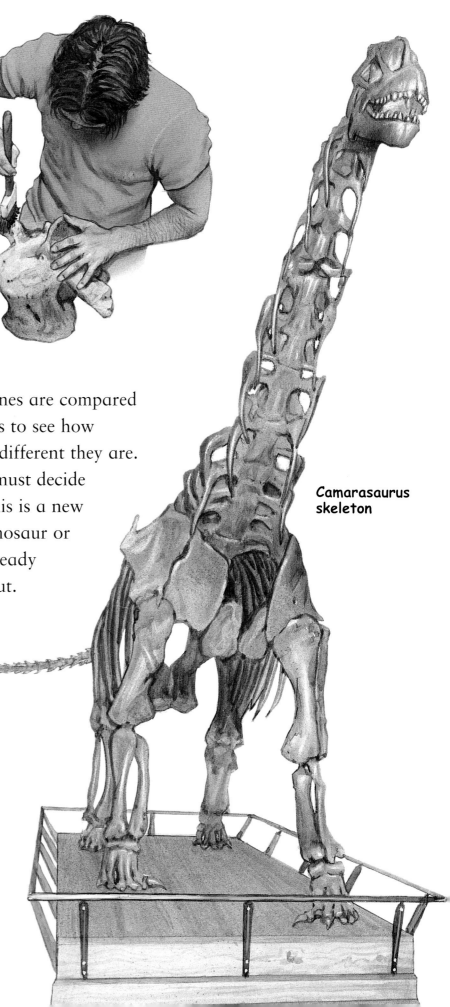

Camarasaurus skeleton

6 ▶ Steel rods or wires are used to hold the heavy bones in position. Plastic bones are made if some of the bones are missing. Once the skeleton has been put together, scientists work out how muscles held the bones together, how skin covered the muscles, and what the dinosaur looked like when it was alive.

Starting a collection

The best way to learn about fossils, rocks, and minerals is to start your own collection.

Keep an eye out for new specimens near beaches, cliffs, and other places where rocks are exposed. Try to find an interesting rock in every place you visit.

Eager explorers

Beaches are great places to hunt for rocks and fossils. Fossils are exposed as the wind and waves wash away soil and plants and break up the rocks. Do not damage or disturb the sites you visit and don't take too many fossils. Always leave something of interest for other collectors to find. Remember to tell an adult before you go collecting.

Displaying

Once you have found some interesting rocks and fossils, clean them carefully. It is very important to make a list of the fossils you have found and where you found them. Try identifying any new finds by looking them up in a book. You can read about their history and label them with the correct names. You can put the best ones on display.

Glossary

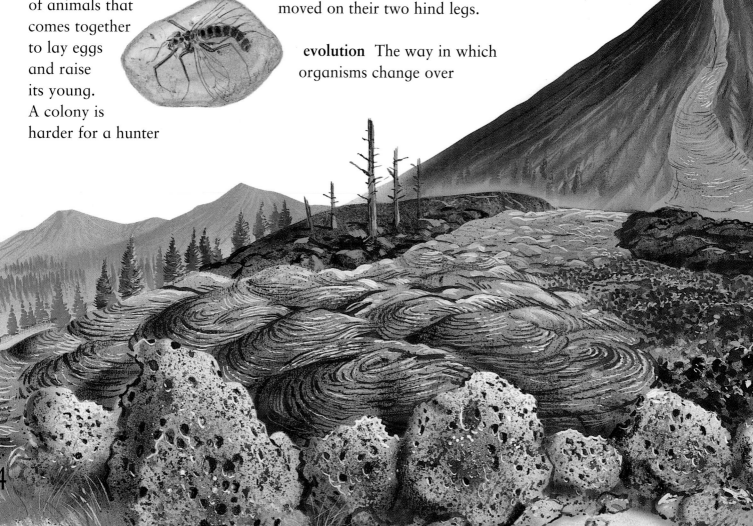

armor A thick layer of bone just under the skin of some dinosaurs— large bone plates in some, smaller knobs of bone in others. This prevented hunters from biting through the skin.

climate The usual, year-round weather of a place. In jungles the climate is hot and wet, in deserts it is dry.

colony A group of animals that comes together to lay eggs and raise its young. A colony is harder for a hunter to attack than a single nest and mother.

core The center of Earth, made of heavy metals.

crust The outer, rocky layer of Earth.

dinosaurs The name for the large land-living reptiles that lived 230 million years ago to 65 million years ago. The name is from the ancient Greek for "terrible lizard."

duckbills A group of plant-eating dinosaurs that had wide snouts like a duck's bill and moved on their two hind legs.

evolution The way in which organisms change over time. Simple life forms have evolved into complex animals and plants.

extinction The death of every last one of a group of plants or animals. The dinosaurs became extinct 65 million years ago.

fossil The remains of an ancient plant or animal. All we know about dinosaurs comes from their fossils.

herd A large group of animals. Many dinosaurs lived in herds for protection—a herd has many ears and eyes to detect an attacker.

lava The hot, melted rock that pours out of an erupting volcano.

meat eater An animal that eats the flesh of other animals, by killing them or by feeding on already dead bodies.

meteorite A chunk of rock that hurtles through space and crashes to Earth. Most are so small that we hardly notice them. The few big ones cause huge explosions.

mineral A mixture of elements, or a single element, which forms crystals. All rocks are made from minerals.

petrification Turning or being turned to stone.

plant-eater An animal that feeds on plants, not on other animals. Most dinosaurs were plant-eaters. So are most animals today.

prey An animal that is being hunted by another animal.

reptile A cold-blooded, scaly animal that lays its eggs on land. Dinosaurs were reptiles. So are lizards, snakes, crocodiles, and turtles.

resin The sticky liquid that oozes from pine trees and hardens to form amber.

rock A mass of mineral material that may or may not be solid.

sauropods The name for all large, long-necked, plant-eating dinosaurs, such as Diplodocus.

skeleton The framework of bones that holds up the body of any animal.

45

Index

A

Albertosaurus (Al-BERT-o-SAW-rus) 22
Allosaurus (AL- o-SAW-rus) 22, 23
amber 33
animals 18, 30, 32, 33, 34, 35, 36
Ankylosaurus (an-KILL-o-SAW-rus) 26, 27
Anning, Mary 38
Apatosaurus (a-PAT-o-SAW-rus) 12, 18
Archaeopteryx 36, 37
armor 26, 27, 44
Avimimus (ah-vee-MIME-us) 30

B

baby dinosaur 8, 10, 11, 14, 15, 40
bone 23, 39
Barosaurus (BAR-o-SAW-rus) 16, 19
bird 30, 36, 37
Brachiosaurus (BRACK-ee-o-SAW-rus) 19

C

Camarasaurus (KAM-ah-ra-SAW-us) 41
Centrosaurus (SEN-tro-SAW-rus) 26
Chasmosaurus (KAZ-mo-SAW-rus) 26
climate 19, 44
coal 33
collecting fossils 42
colony 10, 44
Compsognathus (komp-SOG-nath-us) 28
core 6, 44
Corythosaurus (KOR-ih-tho-SAW-rus) 15
crust 4, 6, 44

D

defense 11, 26, 27
Deinonychus (DINE-o-NIKE-us) 24
Dilophosaurus (DIL-o-foe-SAW-rus) 22
dinosaur claw 8, 24, 29
dinosaur dung 40
dinosaur tail 24, 26, 27, 28
dinosaur teeth 8, 12, 16, 19, 22, 23, 24, 26, 32
Diplodocus (dip-LOD-o-kus) 18, 27
displaying fossils 43
duckbill 12, 14, 19, 44

E

Earth 4, 6, 8, 19, 30, 32, 35, 36
Edmontosaurus (ED-mont-o-SAW-rus) 14, 20
egg 8, 10, 11, 35, 40
evolution 19, 30, 34, 35, 36, 44
extinction 30, 44

F

fangs 23, 24
fish 32, 33, 34, 35
food 11, 12, 16, 19, 20, 23
footprint 18, 20, 35, 40
fossil 32, 33, 35, 36, 37, 38, 40, 41, 42, 43, 44

G

geologist 6, 35, 38, 39

H

hadrosaur 14
herd 11, 12, 14, 15, 26, 28, 44

horned dinosaur 14, 15, 19, 26
hunting 8, 16, 20, 22, 24, 28
Hypsilophodon
   (HIP-see-LOFF-o-don) 29

I
ichthyosaur 38
igneous rock 6
Iguanadon (ig-WAN-o-DON) 14
insect 33

L
Lambeosaurus
   (LAM-bee-o-SAW-rus)
   14
lava 4, 6, 44
Lesothosaurus
   (LE-so-tho-
   SAW-rus) 29
long-necked
   dinosaur 16, 18,
   19

M
Maiasaura (MY-a-SAW-ra) 8,
   10, 11
mammoth 33
mantle 6
meat-eating dinosaur 11, 20,
   22, 23, 28, 34, 44
metal 6
metamorphic rock 6, 7
meteorite 4, 30, 45

mineral 4, 33, 42, 45
museum 38, 40

N
nest 8, 10, 11

O
Oviraptor (OVE-ee-RAP-tor) 29

P
Pachycephalosaurus
   (PAK-ee-KEF-a-lo-SAW-rus)
   14, 15
Parasaurolophus
   (PAR-a-SAW-ro-LOFF-us) 15
petrification 33, 45
plant 8, 10, 11, 12, 16, 19, 30,
   32, 33, 34, 35, 36, 42
      plant-eating dinosaur 12,
         16, 18, 19, 23, 26, 29,
         45
      prey 24, 45

R
reptile 10, 34, 36, 37,
   38, 44, 45
resin 33, 45
rock 4, 6, 7, 32, 35, 39, 40,
   42, 43, 45

S
Saurolophus (SAW-ro-LOFF-us)
   19
Sauropelta (SAW-ro-PEL-ta) 24
sauropod 16, 45
sea 7, 32, 38, 42
sedimentary rock 6, 7, 32
Shunosaurus
   (SHOO-no- SAW-rus)
   19
skeleton 32,

38, 39, 41, 45
Stegosaurus (STEG-o-SAW-rus)
   27
stomach stones 16
Struthiomimus
   (STROOTH-ee-o-
   MIME-us) 28
Sun 4, 30

T
Titanosaurus
   (ti-TAN-o-
   SAW-rus) 18
trace fossil 35
tree 12, 16, 19,
   20, 33, 36
Triceratops (try-SER-a-tops)
   15, 19, 26
Troodon (TRO-oh-don) 8
Tsintaosaurus
   (CHING-dah-oo-SAW-rus) 14
Tyrannosaurus
   (tie-RAN-o-SAW-rus) 20, 22

V
volcano 4, 6, 30

W
weather 32

Places of interest and useful websites

American Museum of Natural History
Central Park West at 79th Street
New York, NY 10024
www.amnh.org

Carnegie Museum of Natural History
4400 Forbes Avenue
Pittsburgh, PA 15213
www.clpgh.org/cmnh

Cleveland Museum of Natural History
1 Wade Oval Drive
University Circle
Cleveland, OH 44106
www.cmnh.org

Dallas Museum of Natural History
3535 Grand Avenue in Fair Park
Dallas, TX
www.dallasdino.org

The Field Museum
1400 S. Lake Shore Drive
Chicago, IL 60605
www.fmnh.org

Natural History Museum of Los Angeles County
900 Exposition Boulevard in Exposition Park
Los Angeles, CA 90007
www.lam.mus.ca.us

New Mexico Museum of Natural History and Science
1801 Mountain Road NW
Albuquerque, NM 87104
www.nmmnh-abq.mus.nm.us

CANADA

Royal Ontario Museum
100 Queen's Park
Toronto, Ontario M5S 2C6
www.rom.on.ca

Royal British Columbia Museum
675 Belleville Street
Victoria, British Columbia V8W 9W2
rbcm1.rbcm.gov.bc.ca

The Hooper Virtual Natural History Museum
www.wf.carleton.ca/Museum

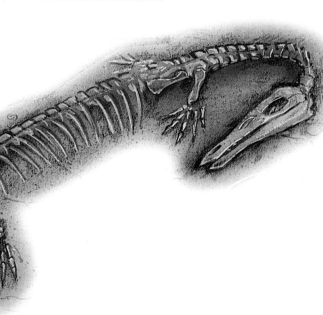